Contents

Some words are shown in bold, **like this**. You can find out what they mean by looking in the glossary.

What is a salmon?

The fish in this photo are called trout. They live only in freshwater rivers.

A salmon is a fish. Some fish live only in **freshwater** rivers or lakes. Other kinds of fish live only in the **saltwater** of the sea.

Egg hatching

4 months

1 year

LIFE CYCLE OF A...

Salmon

Revised and Updated

Angela Royston

www.heinemannlibrary.co.uk
Visit our website to find out more information about Heinemann Library books.

To order:
☎ Phone +44 (0) 1865 888066
📄 Fax +44 (0) 1865 314091
💻 Visit www.heinemannlibrary.co.uk

Heinemann Library is an imprint of Capstone Global Library Limited, a company incorporated in England and Wales having its registered office at 7 Pilgrim Street, London, EC4V 6LB - Registered company number: 6695582

"Heinemann" is a registered trademark of Pearson Education Limited, under licence to Capstone Global Library Limited

Edited by Adrian Vigliano, Harriet Milles, and Diyan Leake
Designed by Kimberly R. Miracle and Tony Miracle
Original illustrations ©Capstone Global Library Limited 1998, 2009
Illustrated by Alan Fraser
Picture research by Tracy Cummins and Heather Mauldin
Originated by Chroma Graphics (Overseas) Pte. Ltd.
Printed in China by South China Printing Company Ltd.

ISBN 978 0 431999 52 4 (hardback)
13 12 11 10 09
10 9 8 7 6 5 4 3 2 1

ISBN 978 0 431999 70 8 (paperback)
13 12 11 10 09
10 9 8 7 6 5 4 3 2 1

British Library Cataloguing in Publication Data
Royston, Angela.
  Life cycle of a salmon. -- 2nd ed.
  1. Salmon--Life cycles--Juvenile literature.
  I. Title II. Salmon
  597.5'6156-dc22
A full catalogue record for this book is available from the British Library.

Acknowledgements
We would like to thank the following for permission to reproduce photographs: Age Fotostock p. **16** (©Paul Edmondson); Alamy pp. **4** (©David Wall), **15** (©Chris A. Crumley), **17** (©Joshua Roper); Ardea p. **19** (©Francois Gohier); ©Corbis pp. **18**, **27**; Getty Images pp. **5** (©Michael Melford), **14** (©Bill Curtsinger), **24**, **29 top right** (©Jeff Foott); istockphoto p. **13** (©Laure Neish); Minden Pictures pp. **9** (©Flip Nicklin), **12** (©Sergey Gorshkov); ©Natalie Fobes pp. **10**, **28 bottom**; Photolibrary pp. **6**, **7**, **8**, **28 top left**, **28 top right** (©Oxford Scientific/Jeff Foott), **20** (©Darryl Leniuk), **23**, **29 top left** (©Digital Vision); Photoshot p. **25** (©Bruce Coleman/Jeff Foott); Shutterstock pp. **11** (©Terry Alexander), **21** (©Oksana Perkins), **22** (©Vera Bogaerts), **26** (©FloridaStock), **29 bottom** (© Xuanlu Wang).

Cover photograph of a sockeye salmon reproduced with permission of ©Photo Researchers, Inc. (Peter Scoones).

We would like to thank Michael Bright for his invaluable help in the preparation of this book.

Every effort has been made to contact copyright holders of material reproduced in this book. Any omissions will be rectified in subsequent printings if notice is given to the publisher.

The bodies of sockeye salmon turn bright red when they grow old.

Salmon are unusual because they live part of their lives in freshwater and part in the sea. This book is about the life of a sockeye salmon.

3 years

6 years

Mating

Eggs hatch out

Female sockeye salmon lay about 5,000 eggs.

In autumn, a female fish laid this nest of eggs. Some eggs have a new fish growing inside them. When an egg is one month old, you can see the fish's eyes inside it.

Egg hatching

4 months

1 year

A tiny salmon with the egg yolk still attached is called an alevin.

This tiny fish has just **hatched** from one of the eggs. The egg **yolk** is still joined to its stomach. It will provide food for the young fish.

3 years

6 years

Mating

4 months

Baby salmon feed near the bottom of the lake.

The young fish has almost finished its store of food. It swims in the **freshwater** of the lake looking for insects and **plankton** to eat.

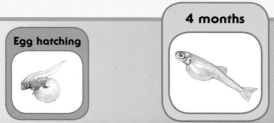

Egg hatching

4 months

1 year

Baby salmon are called fry.

The cold mountain lake is home to millions of young salmon **fry**. Many of the fry are eaten by birds and other fish.

3 years

6 years

Mating

1 year

The young salmon are sometimes called fingerlings. They need to find new food to grow big.

The young salmon are now as big as a human finger. They spend at least one year in the lake. Then they start the long journey to the sea.

Egg hatching

4 months

1 year

Only a few of the young fish will make it this far down the river.

The lake becomes a river, and the river gets wider. The little fish swim under logs and around boats. Many die on the way.

3 years

6 years

Mating

2 weeks later

The young salmon are now called smolt.

The water begins to smell salty, and soon the river flows into the sea. The fish flicks its strong tail and pushes itself through the water.

Egg hatching

4 months

1 year

This seabird has just caught a small fish to eat.

New dangers await the fish in the sea. Young fish are a favourite food for hungry seabirds.

3 years 6 years Mating

6 months later

The salmon's skin now looks silvery.

The salmon swims north into the cold seas around Alaska. It finds plenty of food and grows bigger and stronger.

Egg hatching

4 months

1 year

This young sea lion has caught a fish to eat.

The seas near Alaska are full of seals and sea lion hunting for fish to eat. Our salmon is lucky. It is not caught by a hungry animal.

3 years

6 years

Mating

3 years later

The salmon now have blue-green backs.

The salmon is swimming far out to sea into the deep water. It feeds on shrimp, squid, and small fish.

Egg hatching

4 months

1 year

Some salmon are caught in fishing nets.

This fishing boat is called a trawler. It is bringing up salmon in its fishing nets.

3 years

6 years

Mating

6 years

By now, the salmon is about the length of an adult's outstretched arm.

The salmon is now fully grown. It finds its way back to the river it left five years before. It swims back **upstream**.

Egg hatching

4 months

1 year

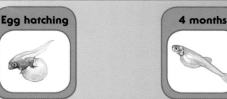

The salmon leaps into the air and flicks its tail.

On its journey the salmon has to jump up **waterfalls**. It jumps as high as it can. Then it swims hard through the rushing water to get over the top.

3 years

6 years

Mating

3 weeks later

The salmon's skin changes colour to bright red.

Many other salmon are swimming up the river too. They are now ready to **mate**. Male sockeye salmon get humped backs at this time.

Egg hatching

4 months

1 year

The salmon do not eat during their long journey, but this hungry bear is about to eat one of them!

3 years

6 years

Mating

2 weeks later

The salmon now have green heads and tails and red backs.

By autumn, the salmon has reached the mountain stream or lake where it was born. Hundreds of other salmon have returned there, too.

Egg hatching

4 months

1 year

This male salmon is ready for mating.

The male fish have sharp, black **snouts** and humped backs. The females are fat with eggs. It is time for the fish to **mate**.

3 years

6 years

Mating

Mating

Salmon nests are called redds.

The female uses her tail to dig a nest in the **gravel** on the bed of the lake. Then she lets the eggs fall from her body into the nest.

Egg hatching

4 months

1 year

Adult salmon leave their eggs after they are laid.

The male swims after her and covers the eggs with his **sperm**. The female flicks more gravel over the nest to hide it.

3 years

6 years

Mating

Journey's end

This bald eagle is grabbing a salmon to eat.

The salmons' life cycle is over. The fish are tired and weak after their long, difficult swim up the river. Some are caught and eaten by hungry animals.

Egg hatching

4 months

1 year

The adult sockeye salmon will die a few weeks after mating.

The rest of the fish die soon after their eggs are laid. In ten weeks' time the eggs will **hatch**. Thousands more tiny salmon will swim in the lake.

3 years

6 years

Mating

Life cycle

Egg hatching

4 months

1 year

6 years

Mating

Journey's end

Fact file

There are seven different kinds of salmon. The sockeye and five other kinds live in the Pacific Ocean. Just one kind lives in the Atlantic Ocean.

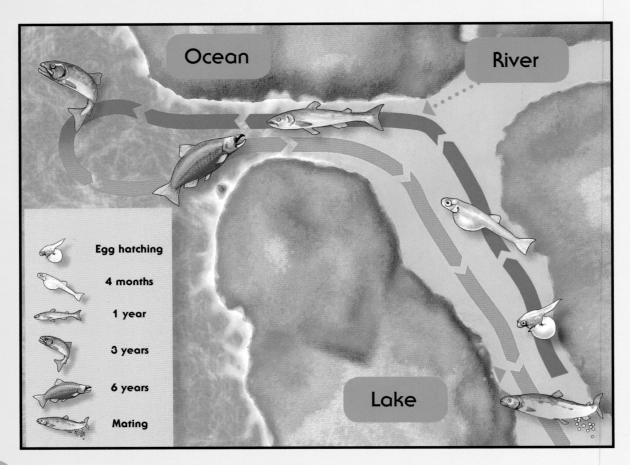

Ocean

River

Egg hatching

4 months

1 year

3 years

6 years

Mating

Lake

Glossary

freshwater water in streams, rivers, and lakes that does not taste salty

fry very young salmon

gravel tiny stones at the bottom of a stream

hatch break out of an egg

mate when a male and a female come together to make babies

plankton very tiny plants and animals that live in water

saltwater sea water contains salt which makes it taste salty

snout the nose and mouth when both stick out together

sperm this mixes with the eggs from the female to make new babies

upstream against the flow of the water

waterfall water flowing and falling over rocks

yolk store of food inside an egg

More books to read

Learning About Life Cycles: The Life Cycle of a Salmon, Ruth Thomson (PowerKids Press, 2007)

Life Cycles: Salmon, Julie Murray (Buddy Books, 2007)

Life Cycles: The Life of a Salmon, Clare Hibbert (Raintree, 2005)

Index